LET'S PLAY
FOOTBALL

Everything You Need to Know for Your First Practice

By Bob Gurnett

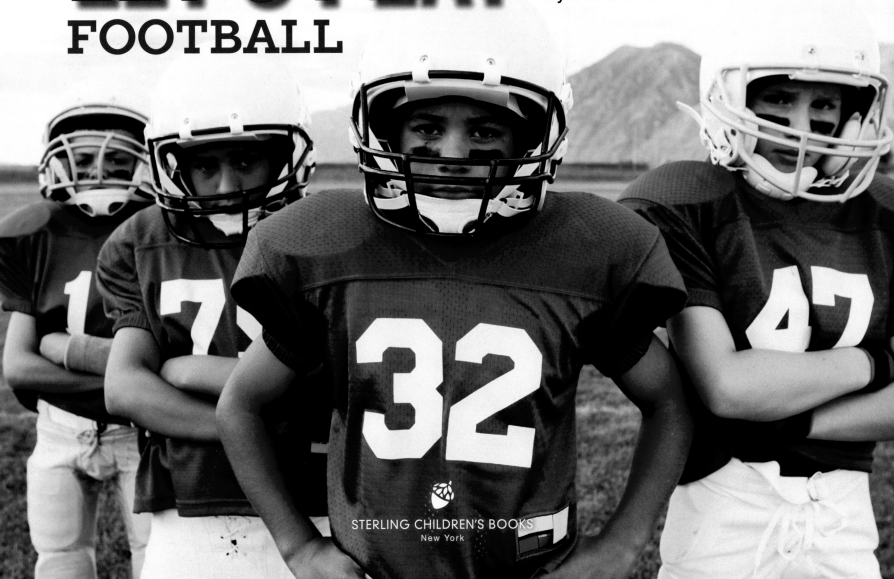

STERLING CHILDREN'S BOOKS
New York

History

Every autumn Friday, Saturday, and Sunday in America is game day! Football started as a game played between rival colleges. It was a modification of the rules of another popular sport, rugby. The first game was played all the way back in 1869! Fans loved watching it so much that professional teams started popping up. In 1920, the American Professional Football Association was started, but you may know it better as the NFL. Almost 100 years later, football is the most watched sport in America. More than 100 million people tune in for the Super Bowl every year. But you don't have to be a professional to play. All you need is a football, pals, and some open space. You may have seen big kids and pros tackle each other, but you can also play two-hand touch or flag football. No matter how you play, the goal is the same: get the ball in the end zone, even if the end zone is the other side of your backyard.

For my niece and nephews—B.G.

STERLING CHILDREN'S BOOKS
New York

An Imprint of Sterling Publishing Co., Inc.
1166 Avenue of the Americas
New York, NY 10036

ISBN 978-1-4549-3204-8

Distributed in Canada by Sterling Publishing Co., Inc.
c/o Canadian Manda Group, 664 Annette Street
Toronto, Ontario M6S 2C8, Canada
Distributed in the United Kingdom by GMC Distribution Services
Castle Place, 166 High Street, Lewes, East Sussex BN7 1XU, England
Distributed in Australia by NewSouth Books
45 Beach Street, Coogee, NSW 2034, Australia

For information about custom editions, special sales, and premium and corporate purchases, please
contact Sterling Special Sales at 800-805-5489 or specialsales@sterlingpublishing.com.

Manufactured in China

Lot #:
2 4 6 8 10 9 7 5 3 1
10/18
sterlingpublishing.com

GLOSSARY

Keep an eye out for these important football terms as you read:

Block—Using your body to get into a player's way to protect a teammate.

Cleats—Special shoes with spikes to get a better grip when running on grass.

Defense—The team trying to stop the offense.

Down—A single play. Each team has four downs to get 10 yards or they give up the ball.

End zone—Each end of the field.

Field goal—Kicking the ball through the uprights. Worth 3 points.

Fumble—Dropping the ball during a play.

Helmet—Worn to protect your head in tackle football.

Interception—A forward pass, thrown to a player on your team, but caught by a player on the other team.

Jersey—A special shirt so you know who is on your team.

Offense—The team with the ball. They try to get the ball in the end zone.

Pads—Worn to protect your body in tackle football.

Pass—Throwing the ball to a teammate.

Penalty—The punishment for breaking any of the rules, usually loss of yards.

Punt—Kicking the ball intentionally to the other team to avoid a turnover on downs.

Rush—Running the ball.

Snap—When the center gives the ball to the quarterback. It means the play has started!

Tackle—Bringing a player with the ball to the ground. Stops the play.

Touchdown—Getting the ball in the other team's end zone. Worth six points.

The Gear

To play a game, you only need a football and room to run. There are different sizes of footballs, but an adult can help you pick out the right size for your age.

The pros wear lot of pads to keep them safe. If you are playing without tackling, all you need is a ball and a lot of space. You can mark the **end zone** with cones or just use your book bags.

Organized teams use more gear, especially when tackling. If you join a tackling team, you will receive an equipment list. This will include a **helmet**, an attachable mouth guard, and shoulder, hip, tailbone, thigh, and knee **pads**.

Some teams have their players wear **cleats**, so they don't slip and fall on the grass. Each team has their own **jersey**, so they can tell who is on their team. No one wants to accidentally tackle a teammate!

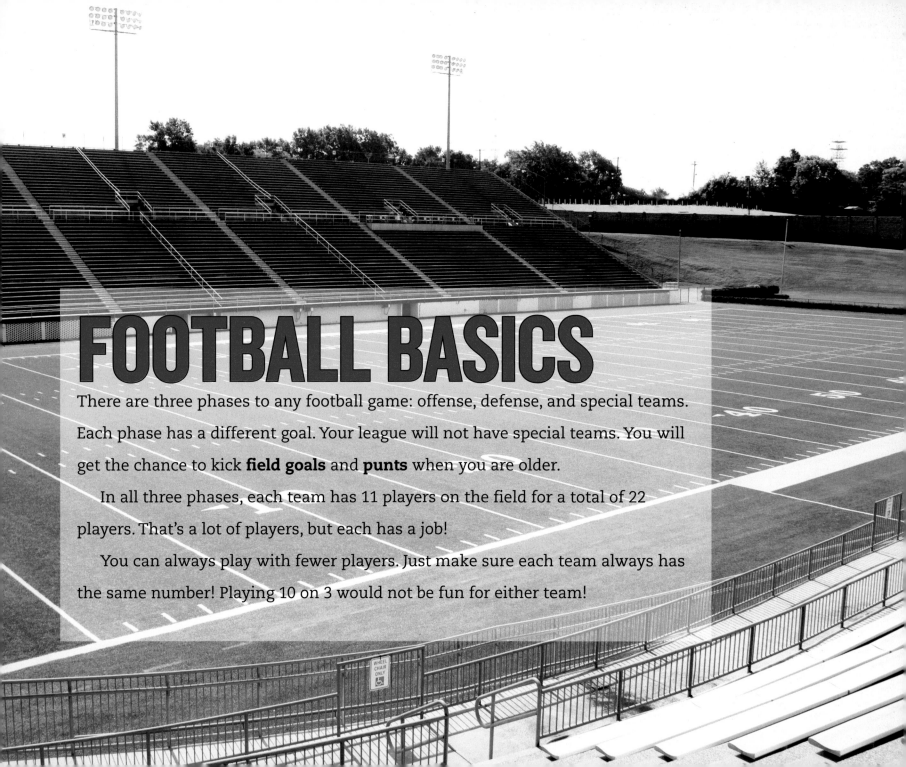

FOOTBALL BASICS

There are three phases to any football game: offense, defense, and special teams. Each phase has a different goal. Your league will not have special teams. You will get the chance to kick **field goals** and **punts** when you are older.

In all three phases, each team has 11 players on the field for a total of 22 players. That's a lot of players, but each has a job!

You can always play with fewer players. Just make sure each team always has the same number! Playing 10 on 3 would not be fun for either team!

Offense

The **offense** has one goal: move the ball into the end zone. They can do it by rushing or passing the ball. They have four tries, known as **downs**, to get it ten yards. If they are successful, they get four more downs to try to go another ten yards. If you get the ball in the end zone, it is worth six points. That is called a **touchdown**!

Here are just some of the things each position does:

Quarterback: Calls for snap, passes the ball, hands off to running back. Leader of the offense.

Center: Snaps the ball, blocks the defense

Offensive line: Blocks the defense

Wide Receiver: Runs down the field, catches passes

Running Back: Runs with the ball, blocks

Tight End: Catches passes, blocks

Rushing

Rushing is when a player runs the ball. It is usually when a quarterback hands off the ball to the running back, but quarterbacks can rush too. Rushing is great for getting small chunks of yards. Be careful, though! If you drop the ball and the other team picks it up, it is a **fumble**. The other team's offense gets the ball where you dropped it.

HOLDING ON TO THE BALL

Remember to practice three points of contact.

1st point: your fingers wrap around and completely cover the tip of the ball.

2nd point: The outside of the ball should be touching your forearm.

3rd point: Press the inside of the ball against your chest. If you think you are about to get tackled, add a 4th point by putting your other hand over the top of the ball. Hold on tight and don't fumble!

Passing

Passing is when the quarterback throws the ball to a receiver. This is a great way to cover a lot of yards quickly! But if the other team catches the ball, that is an **interception**. Your turn with the ball is over, and their offense gets to come out on the field to try to score.

THROWING A SPIRAL

Throwing a football is different than throwing any other ball. A good football pass moves in a spiral and does not wobble. Remember: Your whole body is involved in throwing the football.

To do this:

1. Grip the ball with your fingertips. Don't put the palm of your hand on the ball. Have your ring and middle fingers on the back half of the seams, or laces. Your pointer finger should be close to the back tip of the ball, and your thumb should be underneath the ball.

2. Your feet are as important as your hands. Have the foot opposite your throwing hand facing forward. If you throw righty, your left foot should be facing forward. Your feet should be shoulder-width apart. Make sure to bend your knees a little.

3. Start with your weight on your back foot and when you throw, step into it. Shift your weight to your front foot.

4. Hold the ball up as high as your ear. Your upper arm should be perpendicular to your body. Then move your arm forward in a chopping motion. Now twist the ball slightly and release. Follow through so your hand goes across your body.

It's hard at first, but the more you do it, the easier it is! Don't worry about throwing it far. Get good at throwing a spiral and then worry about aim and distance.

Blocking

How do you get to the other end of the field if 11 people are trying to stop you? **Blocking**. It is the most important part of football! You block by using your body to get in a defensive player's way. This keeps them from tackling the ball carrier. Every player on the offense is expected to block at times, even the quarterback. Never block with your head. You can hurt your head, neck, and upper body.

BLOCKING TIPS

Getting in someone's way is harder than it sounds. To be a good blocker:

- Keep your head up! This is very important.

- Stay in front of the person you are trying to block. Blocking from behind is not allowed.

- Keep a good blocking stance! Feet shoulder width apart, bend your knees, bend at the waist, and keep your back straight.

- Move your feet! If you keep your feet in front the other player, you can keep your balance.

- Keep your head up! It is hard to block what you can't see. It is also safer when you keep your head up!

- Use your hands and arms to push the defender away to make room for the ball carrier. But don't hold onto them! That is a **penalty**.

- If you are on the offensive line, make sure to not stand up to block before the ball is **snapped**! That is a false start and a penalty.

- Keep your head up! It is three times more important than any other tip!

Defense

Your team either scored or turned the ball over. The other team now has the ball. What now? Play **defense**! Your job is to stop the other team from moving the ball forward. Every member of the defense is just trying to stop the ball.

The defense has the same number of players on the field as the offense. Here is what they do:

Defensive Linemen: Stop the run, go after and pressure the quarterback

Linebackers: Get the most tackles, stop the run, help cover receivers, are considered the team's best tacklers

Cornerback: Covers receivers, stops runs on the edges of the field

Safety: Covers receivers, stops big plays, prevents big yardage gains

Tackling

Many types of football, like flag or two-hand-touch, do not require tackling. If you are playing **tackle** football, it is the most important skill a defender learns. It is how you stop the offense. Tackling can also be dangerous. It is important to always listen to your coaches. Do everything they say to avoid hurting yourself or other players.

SAFETY

Be safe! Your safety—and the safety of everyone on the field—is the most important thing when it comes to tackle football. Follow the instructions of your coaches carefully!

- Tackling can be very dangerous if it's done wrong. Make sure never to hit someone with your helmet during a tackle.

- Never grab a player's face mask.

- Never leave your feet when tackling. No diving, no launching.

- Never tackle with your head.

- If you are not sure about something, always ask your coach. No one wants to get hurt.

PRACTICE

Playing football is not just playing the game. To get good, you have to practice with your team. Most teams practice on football fields with the whole team present. There are drills, scrimmages, and other ways to improve your fundamentals.

DRILLS

A drill is practicing a small part of the game to get better at it. Doing the same thing over and over makes you better at it. Just like learning to read or do math, the more you do it, the better you get!

SOME DRILLS YOU MIGHT DO:

Blocking drills: Linemen will block and push against practice pads or other players to work on their form.

Catching drills: Coaches throw balls to the receivers. Sometimes right to them, but sometimes low or high so they can practice catching all over!

Passing drills: Quarterbacks will spend a lot of time throwing at targets or to receivers who are running.

Running back drills: Ball carriers cut around cones to improve their speed and agility, and complete ball security drills to learn how to hold onto the ball and to avoid fumbles. Running backs may have to cut around cones or avoid having the ball stripped by other players.

Tackling drills: Practice safely tackling by going through the tackling motions. Every player will run through drills. That way they are ready during a game.

SCRIMMAGE

Sometimes in practice, the offense and defense will play each other in a friendly game where score is not kept. This is so they can practice combining all the skills they learn in drills.

TIP

Make sure to stay hydrated during a practice. Drink lots of water and stretch with the team before. Practice can be just as tiring as a real game.

To Do:

You don't have to be playing in the game or at practice to get better at football. You can practice by yourself or with friends!

- Run! Run as much as you can! Being fast is a big part of the game!

- Play catch with your friends. Get better at throwing and catching a spiral pass!

- Play two-hand touch and flag football to practice your skills.

- If your team has a playbook, study it!

- Watch what's going on. Stay focused on the action.

- Remember, keep your head up at all times.

Game Day!

What does a game look like? There many different leagues and they don't all work the same way. Check with your coach for exact rules. But here is a very common example.

A game is split into two 22-minute halves. There is a 10-minute break in the middle called halftime.

Your coaches will be nearby while you play. Each team can have two coaches on the field. They will help you remember what to do, and to play safely.

In your league, there probably will not be a kickoff like you see on TV. The offense will start at the 35-yard line.

Every player will get a chance to play in the game, so don't worry if you don't get in right away. Your coach will put you in. Also, don't worry if you get taken out of the game. Every player has to share time with each other. While you are on the sideline, cheer for your team!

Your league might not keep score; that's okay! You are brand-new to football. The point is to have fun and learn the game.

Tips for Game Day!

Here are some tips to make sure you have the most fun on game day!

1. Show up to the field when the coach says! It is okay to be early, but if you are late, you might not get to play.
2. Pay attention to your coaches before the game. They will tell you everything you need to know.
3. Make sure to stretch. Get loose, so you are ready to play.
4. Remember, safety first! If you're playing tackle football, remember to be careful.
5. Keep your head up!
6. Stay hydrated. Make sure to tell your coach if you need a break for water, and let your coach know immediately if you get hurt.
7. Don't get mad or frustrated. Have fun and learn the game. No one is keeping score yet!
8. Play hard, even if the score isn't being kept.
9. The most important thing is to have fun and learn to play. Don't worry if you make a mistake!
10. At the end of the game, shake hands and say "good game" to BOTH teams. Thank ALL the coaches.

A Note to Your Biggest Fan

Parents and caregivers can play a key role in helping kids who are stepping on the gridiron for the first time.

Model model behavior. Teamwork and sportsmanship are critical to any game. Provide encouragement and support to your child, to your child's team, and to your child's opponents. Show respect to the coach and other volunteers.

Let the coaches coach. You have a couple of jobs to do, but coaching isn't one of them. Be sure your child is on time and ready to play, then take a seat and take it easy.

Away from the field, ask the coach to provide practice tips that will support the team methods and message, and privately discuss any concerns you have about your child's playing time or performance.

Temper your temper. As any professional player will tell you, missing a tackle, dropping a pass, and losing are all part of the game. Missteps and missed calls can be frustrating for everybody. Keep cool! The point of football at this level is for your child to safely develop new skills, get some fresh air, play with friends, and have fun. Learning to take mistakes in stride will help your child become a happier, more confident player.